30 Minutes ... To Market Yourself

Tony Atherton

KOGAN PAGE

First Indian Edition 2003
Reprinted 2008

Kogan Page India Private Limited
4737/23 Ansari Road,
Daryaganj
New Delhi 110 002

ISBN-10: 81-7554-220-9
ISBN-13: 978-81-7554-220-4

Published by Vinod Vasishtha for Kogan Page India Private Limited, 4737/23 Ansari Road, Daryaganj, New Delhi - 110 002.

Printed and bound at Print Perfect, New Delhi - 110 064.

CONTENTS

The 30 Minutes Series

The Kogan Page 30 Minutes Series has been devised to give your confidence a boost when faced with tackling a new skill or challenge for the first time.

So the next time you're thrown in at the deep end and want to bring your skills up to scratch or pep up your career prospects, turn to the *30 Minutes Series* for help!

Titles available are:

30 Minutes Before A Meeting
30 Minutes Before A Presentation
30 Minutes to Boost Your Communication Skills
30 Minutes to Boost Your Self Esteem
30 Minutes to Brainstorm Great Ideas
30 Minutes to Deal With Difficult People
30 Minutes to Get Your Own Way
30 Minutes to Get Promoted
30 Minutes to Improve Your Networking Skills
30 Minutes to Make the Right Decision
30 Minutes to Manage Your Time Better
30 Minutes to Market Yourself
30 Minutes to Master the Internet
30 Minutes to Motivate Your Staff
30 Minutes to Negotiate a Better Deal
30 Minutes to Plan a Project
30 Minutes to Solve that Problem
30 Minutes to Succeed in Business Writing
30 Minutes to Write a Business Plan
30 Minutes to Write a Marketing Plan
30 Minutes to Write a Report
30 Minutes to Write Sales Letters

Available from all good bookseller.
For further information on the series, please contact:

Kogan Page India Private Limited
2/13, Ansari Road, Daryaganj, New Delhi-110 002
Tel. 23258325, 23279280, 23283121, 23285874, Fax 0091 11 23267224

1

WHY MARKET YOURSELF?

How do you answer the question, 'What do you do?'

Companies look very carefully at what employees contribute to the corporate good these days, more so than used to be the case. In the 'leaner and fitter' organizations of today, with privatization, fiercer markets and global competition, every employee has to be seen to add value to the organization.

Busy managers may not always remember or even notice work that you are particularly proud of. If they are to know that your contribution is a bit special then you have to find pleasant ways of telling them. After all it is your career, not theirs.

Marketing yourself, in a gentle and gracious way, will help you. Having a memorable answer to the question, 'What do you do?' is a good starting point. It is certainly very good practice for the day when you may want to impress someone outside your company, at a job interview perhaps.

What do you do?

Your answer probably depends on who is asking and what the circumstances are. To a stranger at a party you may give a fairly short and general answer before asking them the same question. To an inquisitive child you give another answer, to prospective parents-in-law still another. To your newly-appointed Chief Executive you would give quite a different answer, with some detail, while still keeping it short enough to prevent his or her eyes glazing over. Most people think up answers on the spot with very little time to think; as a result their words will not be as punchy or as memorable as they might have been.

Some people are prepared for questions like this, especially if they know the new Chief Executive is along the corridor and heading their way. They give memorable answers to such questions. Memorable answers raise your profile and they may produce an invitation to contribute to the more exciting things happening in your organization and so help to build your career.

Such moments can be the decision times in your career when you get to choose between continuing along your current pathway or setting off down a new one that leads onwards and upwards.

For every answer to 'What do you do?' that is interesting and exciting there are at least ten that are dull and uninspiring. What are your answers like?

A training manager might answer:

> I'm the Training Manager. I look after people's training needs, arrange courses, chase people who are late, keep the records, and so on.

Or:

> Me? I help to keep us in business by ensuring that our people have the right knowledge, skills and attitudes in the right place at the right time so that our customers are delighted and come back for more. I'm the Training Manager.

Both answers are accurate in as far as they go, but we hardly need to ask which will be remembered.

Think about how you normally answer the simple question, 'What do you do?' Write down some good answers for different situations and people. Read them out aloud and practise saying them – but do not let it become like reciting a script.

Profile questions

There are many similar questions, sometimes called 'profile questions', and all are variations on a theme – you. Can you give memorable answers to these profile questions? Keep your answers to less than 75 words.

- What do you do?
- Tell me about your career.
- What have you done this week?
- How are things?
- Tell me about yourself.
- What is your proudest achievement?
- What do you have to offer (main strengths)?
- Why do you want a career move?

What is 'marketing yourself'?

Using words like 'marketing' and 'selling' may seem odd when applied to you and your career but they are perfectly valid terms to describe what can be done. Of course, the practicalities of marketing and selling yourself are different from those of marketing and selling petrol or washing powder, although the principles are much the same.

We all know talented and respected people who are passed over in the promotion stakes because they do not 'sell' themselves. We may think we know others who have 'done well' with little talent, who have more froth than substance. Would better self-marketing have helped the former? Did the latter progress with the help of good marketing of a poor product?

It is a truism that, whoever you are, the art of gently marketing and selling yourself (but not being arrogant and pushy) can help you to be more successful in your career – if that is what you want. In this book we look at how you can do this – graciously but successfully. But what does marketing and selling yourself actually mean?

Marketing can be defined as the process of identifying, anticipating and supplying customers' needs at a profit. Selling is the part where you persuade the customer to buy. They are inextricably linked.

You need to both market and sell yourself because your career is a product in a market. Your customer is your employer, especially your manager. Other managers and employers are potential customers. Your product is what you do – hence the stress on the earlier question, 'What do you do?' Marketing therefore involves:

- Understanding your market and how it is changing, knowing what is wanted now and in the future. *What is happening out there?*
- Understanding your current product and changing it to meet future needs, matching it to the market. *What do I have to offer and what will I need to offer in the future?*

- Pricing your product and getting it to the customers. *How much am I worth and where do I want to work?*
- Promoting your product by building customer awareness. *How do I tell and show others what I can do?*
- Selling your product. *How do I convince them?*

Should you market yourself?

You already do. You have already marketed yourself on numerous occasions: you just did not think of it in those terms. You marketed yourself when:

- You tried at school to convince someone to include you in their team.
- You applied for a job.
- You answered an interview question.
- You tried to look smart for a VIP visit.
- You did a job especially well.
- You gave a speech.

If your aim is to be more successful in your career, to achieve fulfilment by using your talents to the full, to climb the ladder of promotion and get more interesting work, then gently marketing and selling yourself is important. As with anything else you will get more benefit if you learn the skills and use them well. So learn the rules and imitate the best; and do it nicely without exaggeration or misrepresentation.

You – a product

In marketing terms you are a product or service and a very complex one at that. You have different aspects to your life and many different roles.

At work you are an employee, perhaps a specialist or professional. Maybe you are also an employer, a manager, supervisor, coach, mentor, leader, counsellor and lots of other things besides.

Outside work you may be a parent, a child, a spouse, an aunt or uncle, a nephew or niece, a friend, a neighbour. Maybe you have a hobby or are a member or an official in a club, society, or church. All of these, and many more, are roles you have in life – aspects of you the product.

Within each role you will have aspirations. To achieve them you need the help of others. At work someone has to pick you for the next exciting project, select you for promotion, delegate to you the next challenging task. How will they know you are interested and able if you do not tell them? Your aspirations may be crystal clear to you but they are as dense fog to others unless you tell them.

How people see you determines how they think of you, whether you spring to their mind when they are looking for someone and whether you are seen as the best choice, an acceptable choice, someone to avoid, or whether you are not thought of at all.

Whether their reaction to you is positive or negative may depend more on what they think of you than on your actual talent. Their image of you comes from you and from others. You cannot control that image but you can influence it.

Selectively volunteering for exciting tasks or projects is a good way to spread the word about you, but you cannot know of every opportunity in your company. The only way you can be considered for roles or posts you are unaware of is for the person in charge to think of you or be told about you. Market yourself and that might happen. Keep quiet and it will not.

Ethics

We have all seen advertising campaigns that are full of hype. Like a soap bubble they are bright and shiny but there is nothing inside. You may have that view of some people whose methods you question. Their methods may be effective for a while but they bring no credit to those involved.

In this book I assume you are good at your profession and want to be even better, using your talents to the full to the benefit of yourself and others. I also assume you want to make legitimate progress in your career while providing a good and professional service to your customer, your employer. You have a good product to promote and you want to do that legitimately and honourably. This is no bluffer's guide.

> **Your self-marketing mission is simply:**
>
> To bring yourself to the attention of others without hype, misrepresentation or false promise.

Be positive

How you describe yourself is very important and we have already seen how your answer to one simple question, 'What do you do?' can leave an image of you that may or may not be helpful.

Consider two contrasting replies to another simple question, 'How are things?' The first is a typical downbeat meaningless reply and you will have heard it, or something like it, hundreds of times. The second is a paraphrase of a reply made by a very successful young manager.

1 'Oh, ok. Muddling through. You know how it is.'

2 'Ever busier. Still expanding. Was in New York last week buying a company. Only a small one but it gets us in the market.'

Of course, you cannot often give a startling reply like the second but you can always avoid negative ones like the first. Successful companies praise their products. Learn from them while avoiding their hype.

Listen to people around you and see how often negative replies are given to the simple 'How are things?' type of question. Always try to give a positive answer: you are describing your product. Include just one or two short facts.

Of course, no one wants a 30-minute monologue in answer to a simple social question. Positive answers can be overdone and achieve the opposite of their intent. Strike the right note by being positive without boasting.

> An extreme example of a negative reply was given by the head of a chain of jewellery shops when he was asked how he could produce such inexpensive silverware. His joke, 'Because it's crap,' led to the demise of his chain of shops and the loss of his name from the high street.

> A housewife and mother of three was asked, 'Do you work?'
>
> Actually, I do work. I'm involved in a programme of social development. At present I'm working with three age groups. First, toddlers: that involves a basic grasp of child psychology and medicine. Second, teenagers. I confess the programme is

not going too well in that area. Third, in the evenings and at weekends I work with a man aged thirty-nine who is exhibiting all the classic symptoms of mid-life crisis – that's mainly psychiatric work. For the whole job you have to be a brilliant planner, have a 'can-do' mentality and have a degree in conflict resolution. I used to be an international fashion model, but I got bored.

(Rob Parsons, *The Sixty Minute Marriage*, Hodder & Stoughton, 1997)

2

ME PLC

It can be enlightening to think of yourself, for a moment, as a company: Me plc.

Companies usually have several divisions or departments that look after various aspects of the business. Typically there will be a production or service department, a research and development group, and departments for administration, marketing, selling and so on. Each of these has a parallel in your career.

Production

What does the production or service department in your company actually do? The people there usually produce the goods or deliver the service for existing contracts. They do this cost-effectively while always looking for ways to improve. As new products are introduced they manufacture them to their traditional high standards, so helping to secure the future while being firmly rooted in the present.

Your 'production' is to keep your present job going as effectively as possible while seeking to improve and respond to changes that occur. For many people this is the height of their ambition and they find it satisfying and fulfilling. Their greatest challenge may be responding to changes but essentially 'production' is about keeping the present role or job.

R&D

A research and development group (R&D) looks much further into the future. They develop the next generation of products. In Me plc this involves deciding what future role or job you want and learning and planning for it – a central aspect of marketing.

R&D means preparing yourself for the next step up the ladder. Can you be one of the first into a new development in your specialism? Should you prepare yourself for management? If you are a manager, can you plan your move into higher management? R&D is all about learning, acquiring new skills, and developing new behaviours and attitudes. Take a wider and longer-term view than you do now and support this with self-development, training and wider experience.

Administration

Administration is about keeping records, maintaining contact with people, and keeping abreast of necessary non-professional changes such as IT. None of it is very exciting and few people actually enjoy it. Do it, but keep it simple.

Records

Keep records of previous jobs and projects – just the main aspects, such as what you did, costs, profit levels and who else was involved. Such details make it much easier later on if you want to describe what you have done to someone, say in an interview.

Record your own training and the things you have learned from projects, jobs, books and so on. Professional institutions call this a professional development record (PDR). If you have not seen one, ask around for a sample.

Keep a list of contacts, simply the name and address, etc, plus brief notes of when, where and why you met.

CV

Keep a record of new achievements in your professional life and update it periodically. This will be very helpful when you next apply for a job in your present company or another one. Use it to update your CV every six months or so.

Marketing and selling

Marketing is about deciding where you fit in at the moment and finding out what the future might be like (market research) and planning the changes you want to make. It also involves 'advertising' – making people more aware of your talents. Selling is about making the changes. The distinction between the two can become blurred but it is what you do that matters, not what you call it.

Conclusion

Seeing yourself as a small company, Me plc, can offer some insights into how to move your career forward. The production people are vital to the success of any company but they do not usually provide the vision that makes it grow. It is tempting to concentrate on production because it is immediate, but if your career becomes 100 per cent production you will only grow by accident.

If you want your career to progress, put time into:

- Finding out what lies ahead (market research).
- Planning and learning for the future (R&D).
- Recording information about yourself and your contacts (admin).
- Marketing and selling yourself.

Action

What specific action have you taken in the last year to improve your 'departments'?

- Production
- R&D
- Administration
- Marketing and Selling

If almost all your action has been in production then you are doing very little to market yourself – as yet.

3

MARKETING

The four Ps

Ask someone who works in marketing what their profession is about and they will tell you about the 'marketing mix' or strategy that consists of the 'four Ps':

- *Product:* Defining the product in terms of what it is, its appeal in the market place, who it is for, what the next generation will be like, how to differentiate it from its competitors, and so on.
- *Price:* Deciding the price or prices.
- *Place:* Deciding how and where to distribute and sell it.
- *Promotion:* Bringing its existence to the attention of buyers by promoting it through advertising and other means.

All four aspects of this 'marketing mix' are important in helping you to market yourself, especially understanding your product (What do you do?) and planning your promotion (How do you tell them you do it?).

To illustrate these four Ps let's imagine we want to launch a new bar of chocolate. We will have to do very well indeed to succeed against established producers like Mars, Nestlé, Cadburys and the like.

- *Product:* Market research will help us to decide, with no guarantee of success, what people say they will buy. Is there room for another Mars type, Kit Kat type, Fruit and Nut type, or any other type? Will it be long and thin or short and fat, a square, a cube or a sphere? What distinctive flavour will it have? Will people break it into pieces like a Kit Kat or bite it like a Mars?
- *Price:* Checking in local shops reveals a wide price range for more or less standard-sized bars of confectionery. How much is charged for image and reputation? Will we undercut the market leader?
- *Place:* How will we get it to the customer? Will we sell direct to retailers or via wholesalers? Will it appear in supermarkets, convenience stores, high street shops, newsagents, petrol stations and vending machines?
- *Promotion:* What image do we want to create (the gentle feminine Milk Tray, the energy-giving Mars, the evening glamour of After Eights)? How will we advertise? Will we associate it with a famous person?

Your product

Thinking of yourself as a 'product' or 'service' can be illuminating. We have looked at the profile questions, 'What do you do?' and 'How are things?' and seen that being prepared for such questions can help you to produce more memorable answers.

In a manner opposite to death by a thousand cuts, small things such as these can help to build your career by a sort of 'climb by a thousand steps'. Of course, we hope there will also be some career jumps along the way – an escalator or two.

Build your career as a climb by a thousand steps, but keep your eyes open for any escalators going your way.

You will expect the profile questions at job interviews but variations can occur unexpectedly in other circumstances and, of course, they can be phrased in a hundred ways. Confident answers help that climb by a thousand steps. They portray a professional image of someone who knows what they are about and can describe it clearly and succinctly.

Most answers you give will fall on stony ground – life is like that – but a few will sow seeds and some of those seeds will germinate and grow. These will bring you into someone's thoughts when they want a good person for a special job – perhaps a move to a new, dynamic and growing department, an escalator going your way.

A toilet cleaner at NASA was asked, 'What do you do?' He is said to have replied, 'I'm helping to put a man on the moon.'

Product life cycles

Every product ever invented has a life cycle. Products are invented and introduced to the market, they grow in sales, reach maturity, sales saturate and then go into decline and finally the product becomes extinct. Unfortunately, so it is with careers.

Some product life cycles are very short, some very long. Some toys are here today and gone tomorrow, whereas the electric light bulb has been with us for over 100 years. What phase of their life cycle would you say credit cards and cheque books are in?

Phases of the product life cycle:

- introduction;
- growth;
- maturity;
- saturation;
- decline;
- extinction.

How does this concept of life cycles affect you and your career?

Think of some products, industries and professions that are at different stages of their life cycles; some examples are shown in Table 3.1.

Your company, your industry and your profession all have life cycles which could be long, medium or short. They are all working their way from introduction to extinction.

What stage do you think each is at now? Tick the boxes in Table 3.2. Could any go into decline or reach extinction before you are ready to retire?

Is the risk high, medium or low that you will have to change your employer, industry, profession, or career?

Table 3.1. Examples of life cycles

	Industry	*Profession*	*Politicians*
Introduction	Bioelectronics	Geneticist	Newly-elected MP
Growth	DNA profiling	PC games writer	Junior cabinet post
Maturity	Electricity supply	Teaching	Senior cabinet post
Saturation	Ship building	Game warden	Elder statesman
Decline	Roof thatching	Bank clerk	Back benches
Extinction	Gas lighting	Stagecoach driver	Lost seat

Table 3.2. Life cycles for your profession, industry, employer and your career

	Your profession	*Your industry*	*Your employer*	*Your career*
Introduction				
Growth				
Maturity				
Saturation				
Decline				
Extinction				

New and improved

Some management gurus believe that many of us will have to change career at least once, perhaps twice, during our working lives. If the stage you have reached in your career life cycle is discouraging, the good news is that life cycles can often be extended. Companies try to extend the life cycle of a profitable product by reinventing it, introducing a 'new-and-improved' version. How many 'new-and-improved' domestic products have you bought?

Here are some examples of extended life cycles:

- Washing powders have the same name as decades ago but the formula has changed many times.
- Pedal cycles have been given a new lease of life as a result of health and fitness and environmental campaigns.
- Old pop songs are re-released or recorded by new singers.

The phases of your career can be extended. Periodically you will need a new-and-improved you, a Mk2 or 3 or 4. You will need to stretch your career, find a new escalator. But first, you need to thoroughly understand your market before you can 'design' this new-and-improved You, Mk2.

Conclusion

In marketing terms you are a product and you can promote yourself by practising answers to some profile questions. All products have a life cycle including your career, employer, industry and profession. Life cycles can sometimes be extended and sooner or later you will need to extend yours. Before planning how to extend it, you need to analyse your market and your current product.

4

ANALYSING YOUR MARKET

To successfully plan for your future, your Mk2, you need to understand the market you are in now and how it is changing. Two widely used tools for analysing markets might be of real use to you. They are the PEST analysis and Porter's five forces.

PEST analysis

This looks at how four external sets of factors might influence the market for a product, in this case your career. Because they are external, you have no influence over them but they can have a strong influence on you. What you can do is watch them, see how they change, try to understand them, and take appropriate action. These external factors are:

- political;
- economic;

- social; and
- technological.

In the case of careers it is worth treating everything as being 'external', including company and departmental issues. Often it is not just one factor in isolation that you need to watch, but the mix of effects from several.

Political factors

What political factors could affect your career, perhaps through your company or industry?

- International politics: regulations, trade agreements and clashes, GATT talks. European rules and directives have changed some industries, for instance fishing.
- National politics: privatizations produce both redundancies and opportunities. Deregulation can put new life into an industry, such as telecommunications. Government initiatives, starting or ending, can change a situation.
- Local politics: planning permission, green-belt areas, new roads. Company plans can fall foul of local regulations.
- Company politics, macro: opening or closure of divisions and factories, mergers and demergers, expansions and cutbacks, core business or diversification. Quality systems. Management fads.
- Company politics, micro: relationships with your boss can affect your career. Is your department stable? Could it be outsourced?

Try to foresee the effects that political movements and decisions are likely to have on your industry, profession, employer and career. What threats and opportunities do they raise? More than one person has made a career out of new initiatives such as ISO 9000 and Investors in People.

Economic factors

What economic factors could affect you? Think about:

- The national and international economies: are they heading for boom or bust and is your industry susceptible to them? (not all are).
- Is your company successful or struggling. Does it have sound financial backing?
- Is your department waxing or waning? Is the budget growing or being cut?
- Has your salary kept pace with the industry?
- How do your company's financial statements compare to those of your main competitors? Compare the Annual Reports.

Social factors

Is your profession or personal career susceptible to social patterns? There is a vast range of them, from divorce rates and one-parent families to out-of-town shopping centres, the rise of supermarket chains, the ageing population, sales of personal computers, the proliferation of mobile telephones, traffic jams, and so on.

Technological factors

Technology changes at an ever faster rate and we soon take new products for granted. Think of some products that were introduced or proliferated only a few years ago that are now taken for granted: call centres, CDs, laser printers, digital television, the tamagotchi, electronic organizers, e-mail, some cancer treatments, many medicines. All were brought about or strongly influenced by changes in technology.

Careers are changed by technology. A typist who will not learn word-processing is unemployable. Mobile phones have created a vast new industry. Technology changes some careers, creates new ones and destroys others. What is it doing to yours?

> **What political, economic, social and technological factors could make an impact on your career, company, profession or industry?**

Spend some quiet time thinking about these four factors and how they can create opportunities for you or pose threats to you. Brainstorm the issues, ideally with a friend. Then take time to think them through and feed your conclusions into your plans for your future.

Porter's five forces

This is another analytical tool used to study markets but with quite a different approach to that of the PEST. It is named after its originator, Michael Porter, and looks at the competitive structure of a market. You can use it to guide your thoughts on the competitive structure of the market for your career.

Michael Porter said there are five main forces that affect the competitiveness of a market. They are:

1 The threat of new people or companies entering the market.
2 The rivalry amongst existing competitors.
3 The bargaining power held by the buyers.
4 The bargaining power held by the sellers.
5 The threat of new substitute products or services.

New entry

Some professions and industries are easier to enter than others. Doctors are well protected, for example, and even have a medical register of who is allowed to practise. Others have less protection or none at all. How easy is it for someone to break into or take over your career?

Are you vulnerable to a threat from others:

- Experienced personnel made redundant elsewhere?
- Newly-qualified college leavers?
- Short-term contractors?
- Part-timers?
- Outsourcing – sub-contracting your department to another company?
- Less expensive staff from poorer countries?

Careers have been attacked and sunk by all of these 'new entries'. How can you repel boarders?

Rivalry

Some industries are cut throat, some are cosy. How much rivalry will there be from your colleagues for your next promotion? How many applicants will come from outside? Is there a policy to promote internally or from outside? Might that policy change? Will others accept different locations, hours, conditions and pay that you will not? How can you counter this?

Bargaining power of employers (buyers)

This increases when there is a surplus of skills in the market place, and drops when there is a shortage. How many good applicants were there when a similar job to yours was last advertised? Ask a friendly personnel officer or apply to an advertised job in another company to find out.

Bargaining power of employees (sellers)

The converse. Your power increases if there is a shortage of people with the required skills and decreases when there is a surplus. Think about how you choose where to buy milk during the day, and where you buy it late at night, when only a convenience store is open. Are you represented by a trade union or do you represent yourself? Which is best in your case?

Substitutes

Substitutes are products or services that could replace yours. They can be complete replacements, such as cars replacing horses or electronic calculators replacing slide rules, or they can be substitute distribution channels such as supermarkets selling petrol and filling stations selling groceries, and both replacing the milkman.

Is there a potential substitute for your career? We have all heard of people who have had to retrain to do other jobs, so it does happen. There are fewer bank clerks today because cash machines and supermarket check-outs have substituted for them. In some companies entire departments have been 'outsourced'. Could it happen to you?

Conclusion

Use the PEST analysis and Porter's five forces to think about your own position, your company's prosperity in its market and you in your market.

See yourself as a seller, supplying a buyer in competition with others, in a market where there could be potential new entrants or threatening substitutes. Identify the main issues. Summarize them in simple terms as opportunities and threats.

What is happening in your market?

5

ANALYSING YOUR PRODUCT

When analysing your product you need:

- details of what it is now, but in more depth than you have had before – your achievements and skills;
- a definition of what you want it to become in response to the changing market, as learned from the PEST and Porter's analyses – your Mk2;
- a plan of how you will move from one to the other – your development plan.

Your achievements

When you need to answer a 'What do you do?' type question in depth it is better to give a 'What I have done' answer. Used to support a description of your product it provides the proof that your product actually works.

Sales people try to impress potential customers with demonstrations or tales of success. You can briefly recount some of your previous successes or achievements to people as needed. This is a case of not hiding your light under a bushel; more than that, in fact – it involves picking the best light to shine to fit the circumstances.

Think back over the last three to five years (beyond that it gets less and less relevant) and make a list of your main achievements, not just the ones you feel particularly proud of, but all of your main ones. Think of what you did, how well you did it, the cost or profit, if relevant, and the time taken, if relevant. Include numbers wherever possible and check them for accuracy.

Later, you can select from these achievements to build better profile statements and even target them at specific people and circumstances by choosing achievements carefully.

When asked, 'What do you do?' expand your answer by describing an achievement that is relevant and easily understood by the person asking the question. This is one reason why keeping good records (Me plc admin; see Chapter 2) is important and why you should update those records with details of recent achievements.

Here are some examples:

- I have coached four of my staff to use the computer system, focusing on what we actually need and saving £600 in consultancy fees.
- I have made a half-hour presentation to the Board for a £100,000 business proposal which was accepted.
- I increased sales in the last quarter by 3 per cent.
- I persuaded Supplier X to give us a 10 per cent discount for the next two years.
- I worked all weekend on the emergency at Customer Y, and solved it for Monday morning.

> List your achievements. Fill several sheets of paper. *This is very difficult, but persevere. Once they start to flow you will get a long list.*

Your skills

You have certain professional skills. Outside your profession these are rare but inside it they are common and do not differentiate you from your competition. Even so, it is useful to ensure that people know about them.

However, some of your professional skills will be unusual. Make a list of these. Your achievements will help you to identify them and provide verification, when you need it, that you really do possess and use them.

> Make a list of your common and unusual professional skills.

Soft skills

You will not enter, let alone progress, in a profession without the basic professional skills, and progression will normally be limited without some of the more unusual skills. Your progression will also be seriously limited unless you possess what are often called 'soft skills', especially the interpersonal skills that relate to dealing with other people.

Use evidence of these soft skills in your answers to profile questions, and examples of when you have used them. In many circumstances these soft skills can be as important as, if not more important than, some of the professional ones. Here are some examples.

Personal skills	*Interpersonal skills*
Creativity	Leadership
Dedication	Empathy
Integrity	Communication
Flexibility	Listening
Copes with pressure	Questioning
Good judgement	Probing
Good intuition	Getting on with people
Uses initiative	Putting people at ease
Self-motivated	Team worker
Positive attitude	Willing to help others
Logical thought	Communicates effectively
Goal oriented	Develops other people
Proactive	Shares credit
Flexible	Motivates others
Makes good decisions	Inspires others.

Classifying skills

It may be helpful to try to classify all the skills you have identified into groups to see if there is a balance. A well-known system, suggested by Richard Bolles, is to use four headings under which to list your skills relating to:

- data;
- ideas;
- things;
- people.

Do the relative size of your groupings suggest some strengths and weaknesses or some areas for improvement?

SWOT analysis

Whether analysing your current situation or planning your future one very useful analytical tool is the SWOT analysis. It might be the most useful analysis you do.

SWOT stands for:

- Your *Strengths*.
- Your *Weaknesses*.
- The *Opportunities* offered in the market.
- The *Threats* posed in the market.

You have two types of strengths and weaknesses:

- *Visible* – the ones other people are aware of.
- *Hidden* – the ones other people are not aware of.

SWOT works best when applied to a specific issue rather than in a global, unfocused manner. To do this focus on specific issues you are facing and SWOT them one by one. Take larger or more global issues and break them down into parts and SWOT the parts. Here are some examples of subjects to SWOT:

- How well do I match my current market?
- Should I apply for the new opening in Department X?
- I need to be noticed more by the decision makers.
- It looks like we will be bought by/will buy Company X; what should I do?
- There is to be a new project team; should I apply?
- I have a new boss; what should I do?
- There is a major reorganization coming; how should I react?

Table 5.1. Example of SWOT analysis: my company has just been taken over

Strengths	*Weaknesses*
I am well thought of in this department	All my experience is with this one company
I am working on a long-term project	I know very little about the new company
That project is profitable	I have never led a full project
I am adaptable and flexible (hidden strength)	I struggle with the financial side (hidden weakness)
I have a new project management certificate	
Opportunities	***Threats***
New merged company is bigger	There will be some redundancies
We are expanding abroad	They are already strong in my area
Our new owner specializes in projects	The customer for my current work does not like the take-over
There will be new work groups formed	If they move our offices to theirs, it is 50 miles away and I hate commuting
There is a shortage of my skills outside	

Use the SWOT analysis as a general-purpose tool to attack any problem.

- *Strengths.* What are your strengths relevant to this problem? Are they known to others? How can you reveal your hidden strengths?

- *Weaknesses.* What are your weaknesses relevant to this problem? Are they known to others? How can you improve them?
- *Opportunities.* What opportunities are there? What were identified through the PEST and Porter's analyses?
- *Threats.* What threats are there? What were identified from PEST and Porter?

The SWOT plan

Once you have completed a SWOT analysis use it to develop a plan to:

- match the opportunities to your strengths;
- make hidden strengths visible;
- minimize the threats or turn them into opportunities;
- improve visible weaknesses, turn them into strengths;
- improve your hidden weaknesses.

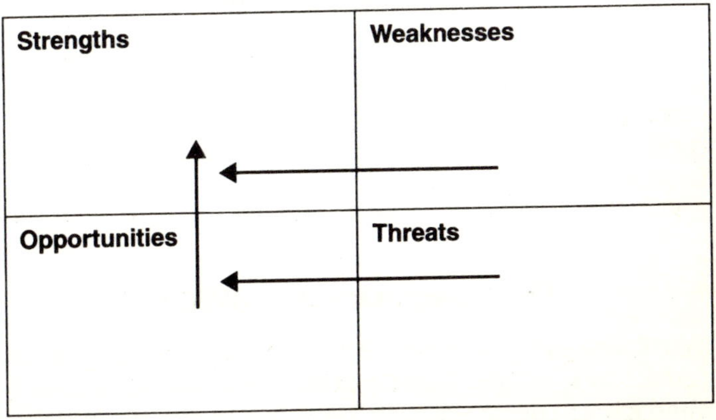

Figure 5.1. Turn weaknesses and threats into strengths and opportunities

Use SWOT analyses liberally and quickly. The more you use them the better you will become and the more useful they will be.

Definition of You Mk2

Now that you have learned more about yourself as a product and the market you are in, you are better able to define what you want to be in the future, say in three to five years time. Try to define what you will be in terms of:

- professional or specialist competence;
- managerial competence;
- position in the hierarchy;
- salary level.

Make your definition as specific as you can and give it a deadline. Consider alternative scenarios.

Development plan

Now you can seriously plan for your personal development (Me plc R&D; see Chapter 2). Look not just to strengthen current weaknesses but to build strengths for your future career position, your Mk2. Ensure that you have specific targets and the means of judging if they have been achieved, together with deadlines for when to achieve them.

The competition's SWOT

SWOT analyses can also be used to analyse your main competitors. Do the SWOT just as you would for yourself, although of course you will know less detail about them. Then plan what you have to do to compete with them.

6

PRICE

In comparison with defining your product, pricing your career is relatively straightforward. It involves not merely your salary, though that is likely to be the most important aspect, but also any perks you can reasonably expect to go with the job.

You are a cost

The cost to a company of employing you is greater than the cost of your salary because there are a number of overheads. Very roughly, you can say that it costs a company £10 an hour to employ you for every £10,000 of your annual salary. This allows for holidays and weekends, a 37-hour week, and a significant contribution to overheads.

Adding value

You can add value to a company either by bringing money in or preventing it from going out, ie by helping them to earn more or spend less. For the company to make a profit from you, on average you need to earn or save for them more than £10 for every £10,000 of your salary, every hour. If you exceed that figure then you are a financial contributor to the company, if not then you are a financial drain.

Knowing how much value you add to the company can be a very helpful statistic. It certainly gives a flavour to your achievements and demonstrates your eye for business, and adds zest to your answer to, 'What do you do?'

> Two accountants were asked what they do for the business. One said, 'I look after the books, check the figures, keep the finances ticking over.' The other replied, 'The most important thing I do is to make absolutely certain we get the cash flow right. Get that wrong and we're bankrupt no matter how full the order book is.' Which reply gets remembered?

Your price

Pricing policies can be very complex and determining salaries is no different. The company must make a profit out of you either by paying you less than you add or less than you save.

Personnel officers have access to guides and information that enable them to compare your salary to that of others inside and outside the company, but some jobs are hard to get comparisons for.

You can make your own comparisons, but be realistic. Here are some ideas:

- Swap details in confidence with people at similar levels in other departments or other companies.

- Consult salary surveys, especially those from professional institutions (read the fine print to see what is included).
- See equivalent government positions; their salary bands are published.
- Monitor job advertisements – those as close to your own as you can find.
- Try the internet for job advertisements and surveys.
- Check perks: pension (contributory or non-contributory), accident insurance, medical insurance, car or allowance, petrol allowance, financial loans, bonuses, profit sharing, share or stock scheme, leisure facilities, subsidized lunches, and so on. Ask about the cost of each perk as they are all part of the gross pay.

Once you have the true picture then you may start to plan your argument for a pay rise or a move. Without the true picture, the counter-argument will wipe you out.

Differential pricing

If you are self-employed you may find that you have to charge different prices to different customers. This is a common practice and is called differential pricing. For example, the cost of a railway ticket is different for pensioners, students and commuters, and changes with the time of day.

7

PLACE

The third P, place, refers to the distribution channels used to get your product to the customer. Thinking of your career, place can refer to a variety of aspects of where you work; things such as:

- geographical location: country and county, town or countryside;
- time and distance taken to travel to work each day;
- type of organization: commerce, industry, retail, charity, etc;
- size: small, medium, large, national, multinational;
- headquarters or branch office;
- ownership: private, public, stock market quoted.

You might think some of these are important to you, others not. How might they affect your career?

- A large company may offer training with formal qualifications.
- A large company may offer the chance to move around.

- A large company may offer large or prestigious projects.
- You may like the idea of working for a famous company.
- A small company may offer greater flexibility of work and provide rapid and wide experience.
- A small company may offer rapid promotion as they expand.
- Travelling a lot each day to and from work may prevent you from gaining extra qualifications at evening class.
- Commuting can be very expensive.
- In a small company you will get to know everyone.
- In a large company you may feel like just a cog in a machine.
- You may get shares in a private company.

There are many variations. What do you want?

8

PROMOTION

In marketing terms promotion is not about moving to a more senior job: it is the art of bringing your product to the attention of potential buyers, in effect – advertising. It is not actually selling, although it may include what many people would regard as 'selling themselves'.

Objectives

The objectives of promotion can be summed up as:

- to increase the customer's awareness of your product or service;
- to convince them of its importance to them;
- to remind them of how it is different from its rivals.

You will probably want to make senior managers more aware of you and the contribution you make and can make to the company (your potential), and to remind those with whom you have worked before. You will need to list the people you are targeting. Also try to raise the awareness of your work outside the company.

No matter how excellent you are some of your colleagues will be just as good, if not better, at some aspects of your work. Remind your target audience of your particular strengths and your specialist skills. Remind yourself by revisiting your SWOT analysis and your achievements.

Avoid criticizing your competition. Competing with your colleagues for a promotion is a temporary situation; you still have to cooperate with them the rest of the time. Good managers will always look for cooperative team players.

Avoid gross exaggeration. The 'buyer beware' saying should not apply to you. Your buyers should not need to be wary: they have entrusted you with their business. Remember your mission as suggested in Chapter 1:

> **To bring yourself to the attention of others without hype, misrepresentation or false promise.**

Before we look at the methods you can use to promote yourself it will be as well to know who you are aiming at.

Target audience

There are two broad types of target audience: those you reach with a scatter-gun and those you reach with a sniper rifle.

Television advertising is a scatter-gun approach. It reaches a large number of unknown people even though aimed at specific groups such as children or adults. Your scatter-gun could include writing articles for specific magazines or journals and giving a presentation at a conference.

Direct mail is an example of the sniper approach. It is targeted at known people and often addressed by name. Sniper fire for you might be to go to meetings attended by specific people you want to reach, or to write a report for the Board or senior managers.

Sniper fire

Sniper fire is likely to be the most useful approach for you. Your ideas of where you want to get to, the You Mk2, should help you to think of the people who may be able to help you along the way. Without that work, targeting your promotional audience is going to be less effective than it could be.

Of course serendipity and chance play a part. But those who are well prepared are more likely to make good use of opportunities presented by chance than those who are not. This is what people mean when they talk about 'creating their own luck'.

Inside and outside your company, who are the people who could help to foster your career? Who can open opportunities to you and encourage you to use your abilities to the maximum? You need a stage on which to operate. Who controls access to the stage? Who selects the cast? Who can:

- Pick you for . . . a new team?
- Suggest your name for . . . a new project?
- Support your inclusion in . . . a committee?
- Tell you about . . . special tasks?
- Who can coach you in some special skill?

Motives

Again, a word about ethics. What is your motive for looking for help like this? Is it to become a contributing member of a higher team so that you can use your talents more fully? Or is it to claw your way over others? We all 'use' people to some degree but to what extent do we repay that use? Are you as willing to help as to be helped? If you are engaged in a two-way process of mutual help, even if your help is directed at a third party, then you are likely to have little to worry about from an ethical viewpoint.

Your sniper's list

So who is on your sniper's list? Think of people inside and outside your organization. Take any legitimate opportunity to meet the Chairman, the Chief Executive and any Director or head of division, including Personnel. If you are naturally reticent, practise your profile statements and try to be a little bolder, but do not become Attila the Hun.

Consider people you know in:

- your department: colleagues, subordinates, manager, manager's manager;
- neighbouring departments;
- other groups, sections, branches, sites;
- your professional life: acquaintances at meetings, committees;
- your suppliers and customers: the representatives you meet.

If appropriate, consider your family, friends, neighbours and other acquaintances.

Remember your colleagues and those in other work groups who can tell you what is going on, those who make up the grapevine. Often the grapevine will provide accurate information before the formal chains of communication grind into action.

Once you have your target list you can decide how to communicate, and what methods to use to promote yourself. Update the list from time to time.

When you approach people avoid asking for a favour. Usually it is better to ask for information or advice than for action. If they want to take action, let them volunteer. With your manager, you do the volunteering.

Scatter-gun approach

Your scatter-gun targets will be less well defined. Your objective is to reach people you have never met, mainly outside the company but not exclusively, people outside your circle. Your aim is to get your name known in your profession or industry.

There are various ways to do this. For example, you could make a presentation at a conference or simply attend a conference and meet people during the coffee and lunch breaks – this is a very common and successful way of meeting new people from within your profession. You can put your name in front of even more people, but without meeting them, by writing an article or even a letter for a specialist magazine.

Your scatter-gun targets are not specific people but groups of specific people at the places where they meet or correspond. Make a list of your possible scatter-gun targets such as:

- specialists and other professionals;
- people in other parts of your company;
- senior managers.

And where you can reach them:

- specialist magazines or journals;

- your company magazine;
- professional institute committees or meetings;
- other meetings;
- conferences: organizing, addressing or attending;
- action groups;
- as a company representative to . . .

Promotional methods

You are likely to use four types of promotional methods: the spoken word, your actions, your appearance, and the written word. You also need to be aware of your 'branding' and how you can influence it.

The spoken word

Your spoken words are one of the prime means of promoting yourself to other people. There are three main ways in which your spoken words are noticed: the times when you use your profile statements, the occasions when you make a presentation, and every time you speak and portray either a positive or negative image of yourself.

Profile statements

The profile statements we looked at earlier are important. They all derive from the 'Who are you?', 'What do you do?' and 'How are you?' base questions. Make your answers as pleasant, interesting and memorable as possible and not too long.

If you have already written some first attempts revisit them now and try to improve them. Can you include an achievement or two, with a couple of memorable facts – the proof of the pudding? Practise saying them out loud. Do they sound pompous or self-centred? Update and improve them periodically.

Presentations

Take any opportunity to make a presentation, provided of course that you know what to talk about and will not make a fool of yourself. There are three reasons why people shy away from making presentations:

1 They do not know the subject matter, or a colleague knows it better.
2 They lack presentation skills.
3 They are fearful of standing up and addressing a body of people.

All three are valid reasons but ideally you should only miss an opportunity because of the first. The other two can be addressed by attending training courses or reading books on presentation skills.

Should it be part of your development plan to either read books on presentation skills or attend a training course?

There are two secrets to making a good presentation. Together they improve your performance and reduce, but do not eliminate, the butterflies. They are:

1 Thorough preparation.
2 Careful practice.

No matter how experienced you are at making presentations you should still practise beforehand when a new or particularly important presentation is to be made.

Making a presentation gives you a wonderful chance to make an impression on people, hopefully a good one. Inside your company you could be addressing senior managers or the Board. At an external meeting you could be addressing other professionals. All will give you 100 per cent attention for the next few minutes. A born sales person would eat their heart out for an opportunity like that. Do not miss it even if you are nervous. Often you will get opportunities for one-to-one conversations afterwards; use those as well.

Opportunities to prepare and make presentations are relatively common. If you really want to you should be able to make several a year, and each one puts you in the limelight, so they do need to be good.

Look to see what external opportunities there are, such as at conferences, professional meetings (national or local), sales presentations, and so on. Improve your skills with in-company presentations first. Helping on internal training courses is one way of getting some practice.

Every time you speak

One manager I used to know was very competent at his job but whenever I met him I could guarantee he would give me every negative slant to the latest company change or initiative. Even when saying something positive his body language and tone of voice would be negative. Do you know people like that? What impression do they make on you? Might anyone be thinking of you like that?

Whether you try to or not you create an impression whenever you meet and talk with anyone else. That impression has two aspects: professional competence and personality. Their view of you rests not just on what you say but on how you say it. Every conversation contributes to whether someone sees you as:

- professionally competent or incompetent, and
- personally positive or negative.

Next time you are listening to someone on television, perhaps a politician, or a chat-show guest, or a news reporter, take note of how their behaviour influences you as much as their words. Notice their posture and stance, their facial expressions, their demeanour, the intonation of their voice and their choice of words.

Why not try to cultivate a positive and cheerful manner to go with your professional competence? Imitate the best.

Actions

The best advertising is a personal recommendation. So first and foremost you must perform *a good, professional job,* keeping up-to-date as necessary. That will help your Me plc Production department to keep going. Remember that you do not need to be the best to be successful; by definition not everyone can be the best. But life gets easier when you are noticeably better than average.

> An engineer was made redundant after 20 years with the same company. His prospects looked bleak but he sent speculative applications to people he had met through his work. 'We thought about poaching you last year,' said one as they offered him a job, 'but we didn't want to upset your employer because they're our best customer.' The moral: the good impression you create by doing a good job may one day come back to serve you.

Second, stretch and *expand your professional skills.* Keep pace with the present (Me plc Production) and build for the future (Me plc R&D and You Mk2). Your personal development plan should include:

- training to learn new knowledge and skills or improve existing ones;
- coaching from those who can do things you want to learn, and coaching others;
- teaching yourself from books, CD-ROMs, videos and learning packages;
- learning from experience by volunteering for new tasks and projects.

Third, *develop your soft skills;* those personal and interpersonal skills that we highlighted earlier. When recruiting new staff it can be relatively easy to find people with the specialist knowledge and skills. Often it is much harder to find someone who can handle people and get the best from them. People skills can be the hardest to find so develop yours to the full.

Fourth, *look out for escalators.* If you have been involved in one challenging project you will want another one. Get into the newer and expanding areas of your company and get out of the older, shrinking areas. All companies have both; it's up to you to choose. Again, volunteering is the way. If you are given a task that is an old cabbage this time, complete it with a smile while trying to get a promise of a peach next time.

Fifth, to use a horrible word – *network.* In plain language, keep in touch with people, especially those who may be able to help you through advice and information – your sniper targets. And be sure to help them and others whenever you can, not so that they 'owe you a favour' – a very selfish attitude – but because that is what you are here for. In any case, being known as a helpful person is a desirable image.

Sixth, *associate with others.* At work it is natural to lunch with your immediate colleagues. Branch out and lunch with people from other departments and work groups. Listen to what is going on outside your group.

Finally, *be associated with success* – not as a hanger-on but as a contributor. To use that old saying, don't be a passenger be part of the crew – preferably the captain or navigator.

Appearance

Always try to look the part or slightly above it. In other words dress to suit the image of the successful person doing your job, or slightly better.

Knowing what this image is can sometimes be difficult. If you were going to an interview for a new job you would automatically dress to suit your image of the new position. Take note of how those senior to you dress and decide if you would like to imitate them. As in other areas, imitate the best if you are going to imitate anyone.

> In Hong Kong in the 1980s, then a British colony, some Chinese bankers dressed in pin-striped suits, wore bowler hats and carried rolled umbrellas. It looked like the City of London except that the humidity was in the 90s and the temperature was in the 30s (90s Fahrenheit).

> A well-established, dynamic British firm was bought by a youthful American firm. The American code of 'dress down' (jeans and tee shirts) flew in the face of the previous 'professional' look and almost caused hysteria. How many careers were damaged, unintentionally, by the feeling that they were 'not one of us'?

The written word

Every article, report, letter, memo and e-mail you write says something about you. They speak of your professional and technical competence and they portray an image that depends on your skill at writing. This image is portrayed both inside and outside the company.

Not everyone is naturally blessed with good writing skills. If you are not then try to approach your writing in three stages:

1 *Preparation.* Increase the time you spend preparing your material before starting to write. Gather your material together, organize it and sequence it first.

2 *Writing.* Write without stopping to make corrections (except for minor mistakes). This is a creative time so do not stop to criticize your work.

3 *Editing.* Now criticize it. Look for ways to use simpler words and shorter paragraphs. Check grammar and spelling and get someone who is good at grammar to check it for you. Good secretaries are ideal.

Books

Writing a successful professional book will get your name noticed, but it is a difficult feat to achieve. Most submissions to publishers are rejected. Note that:

- it needs a huge investment of your time, with no guarantee of success;
- you should write a letter to the publisher first; send a synopsis, a list of chapters and a sample chapter;
- check in bookshops for which publishers are publishing your type of work;
- tell your employer: they might help with facts and illustrations;
- you must not give away the business's secrets.

Articles

Target the magazines and journals that publish the type of articles you can write and are read by the people you want to reach inside and outside your company.

- Check the typical length and complexity.
- Check the style including sentence lengths, complexity of the words and jargon.
- Check their use of illustrations and photographs.
- Send a proposal rather than a manuscript and ask if they have guidelines for authors.
- Tell your employer and get any help they will give.

Reports

Reports may be internal or external. Many people dislike writing reports and your boss may welcome a volunteer. Make sure you are professionally happy with the content and try to ensure that your name goes on the cover along with his or hers. Write brief reports on your own work whenever you can. Sometimes reports are delivered with a verbal presentation. That may open an opportunity for you to make the presentation and join in the subsequent discussion.

Letters, memos, faxes and e-mail

Treat each one in a professional manner.

- Letters will usually be on good quality paper with a company letterhead and logo, both of which look professional and add authority.
- Memos are for internal use and may be less formal than a letter. Make yours slightly more formal than average so that they are more noticeable.

- Faxes and e-mail may be printed on cheap paper by the recipient. They may not have a company header or logo and so you have only your words to display your professionalism.

CV

Your CV is an advertising leaflet and exists only to promote you. Use your CV more widely than is traditional. Use it to promote yourself internally when you try to join another team or group as well as when applying for jobs outside the company.

- Include some of your achievements as proof of your ability; do not just list responsibilities.
- Focus on the last five or six years with only an outline of previous experience to show career development and continuity of work.
- Keep your standard CV up to date.
- Use no more than two pages of A4 white paper.
- When applying for a job rewrite your standard CV, focusing it on the particular job.

Branding

Branding is used to give a product an identity, to make it different from its competitors and secure customer loyalty. It is very powerful. For example some supermarket customers will ignore 'own brand' products, even when reduced to silly prices, in order to buy the traditional brand they have come to trust. The same can be true at work when managers are selecting a team for a prestigious new project and choose their old favourite people.

You already have a 'brand' whether you want one or not because branding exists in other people's views of you. You need to be aware of how people have branded you or 'see you' and, if necessary, influence them to re-brand you in a different way.

Branding can be a serious career problem after a company merger or a change of job. 'Old' staff quickly form impressions of what 'new' people are like: they are branded. There is a feeling of 'us and them' which lingers for a long time because of the different original cultures.

As two organizations merge occasions inevitably arise when managers have to select staff for a new project or post. When they favour staff from their old company, even if trying not to, that is branding. You may say they are simply choosing those they know best or know they can trust. Fine, but that is branding.

Here are some examples of people who are easily branded:

- students, young people, the over-50s;
- ex-forces personnel and ex-civil servants;
- headquarters staff;
- field staff.

Genuine quotations that reflect branding:

- About Research and Development staff: '*They're different in R&D*.'
- About the company accountants: '*They live on a different planet*.'
- About staff from the other company after a merger: '*They're a funny lot*.'

You are already branded to some degree. People already feel some sort of loyalty to you or not, they already feel some trust in you or not, they already feel some preference towards you or not. You can affect this image, this branding, in the ways described above by consciously trying to shift the image from a clone of Company A or B to a personal image or brand of you: Me plc.

Use the things you say and do to disassociate yourself from any negative images attached to your division, your group, even your profession (while retaining personal friendships and loyalties) and associate yourself with positive images by demonstrating your individuality and originality.

The best positive brand you can have is success, which brings us back to the general advice to: *Imitate the Best.*

Conclusion

Promotion is about increasing peoples' awareness of you so that they are more likely to 'choose' you. Use both sniper and scatter-gun approaches to reach your selected targets using the spoken word, the written word, your appearance and your actions. Identify and change any negative 'branding'.

9

SELLING

During or after every marketing campaign there comes a time when someone has to sell the product or service to a real customer. You too will face such occasions. These could be at a formal interview for a new job, or when meeting someone who is putting a new team or department together, or when meeting a senior manager whose group is expanding, or other similar situations. In all of these cases you will need to 'sell yourself'.

The six stages of selling

It is said that there are six stages in personal selling.

1 Gaining entry to the potential customer – the decision maker.

2 Identifying the needs of the customer.

3 Matching the features of your product or service to their needs.

4 Selling the benefits of your features by describing what the customer will experience.

5 Answering the inevitable objections that customers raise.

6 Closing the sale: moving them from intent to action.

These sales techniques are worth knowing about. Apart from being useful when defending yourself against a pushy sales person, they can be applied to furthering your career. Consider the most challenging example: a formal job interview.

Gaining entry

Your promotion efforts (the application letter, application form and CV) have gained an invitation. If it is an internal post you will have reminded the manager of achievements that he or she already knows about, plus some that are new to them.

Identify needs

The homework you did on the company and the job, coupled with carefully listening to what the interviewer tells you, should give you a picture of the customer's needs. When unsure of a point or two – ask. With an internal post quiz people you know in the department before the interview. What have been the successes and failures of this group? What new contracts and problems do they face? How will they approach them? Why has the new post been created?

Match features to needs

Mentally check how your knowledge, skills and attitudes/behaviours (such as dedication, motivation, etc) fit what is needed. Identify the key points in your mind.

Sell the benefits

Explain to the interviewer how your skills and experience provide what they are looking for. Relate to their problems by describing relevant achievements in your past and let them think about how similar successes could make life easier for them.

> Your situation here sounds similar to one in my last job. I devised a new system and implemented it. In the first year we reduced waste by 12 per cent, which was more than had been achieved in the previous three years.

Handle objections

Ask if there is anything they are not sure about. Are they satisfied that you have the necessary skills and experience and can do the job? Have they any reservations about offering you the job? (Can you really ask that? Yes!)

Close the sale

This is not always possible at a real interview – there may be other interviewees sat outside waiting their turn. Tell the interviewer that you still want the job, and why. Ask them when they will decide and when ideally they would like you to start. Let them know that you have other options but that this is your preference.

Selling the benefits is the most difficult stage apart from closing the sale. Look beyond the immediate problem to show how you can make life easier or better for them. You are professionally competent but so are all your competitors. How you sell yourself as a solution to their problems, and how well you will fit in with their team, are often the deciding factors.

> Analyse television advertisements to see how they sell to you. Any motor car will get you from A to B, any washing up liquid will clean your dishes, any bank will provide a credit card; so how do they try to persuade you that they are different from all the rest?

Sell the benefits you can bring, not just your skills. To paraphrase a once-famous television advertisement for sausages: sell the sizzle, not the sausage.

Referrals

Good sales people always ask for referrals, that is for the names of other people who might be interested in their product. Listen for the names of people who might be interested in you. Ask for 'referrals'. The best advertising is by word of mouth.

Conclusion

Learn the basics, the six stages of selling, and see how they can be applied to marketing you. Concentrate on 'selling the benefits, not the features' – the sizzle, not the sausage.

10

CONCLUSION

Personal satisfaction lies, at least in part, in using your talents to the full to achieve things for yourself and for others. Marketing yourself helps you to do that. It is nothing new. You have been doing it for years even if you didn't realize it.

Approached in the right spirit, gently and with integrity, it can help to build your future and fulfil your potential.

So, 'What do you do?'